The Penultimate Poems

first edition —rev a

Joseph Leo Hickey

Cover artwork by Michael Thompson with background image from Pixabay.

Melodium
House

www.MelodiumHouse.com
joseph@melodiumhouse.com

The following group of poems were sent to the email inbox of every student at a high school years ago by a student named Serenity, after her first day there. This group of poems was only widely read after her death. And only after she was murdered, did these poems gain recognition. People assigned new meaning to each of them.

1

some nights i wake up
just to look out and see the stars

some nights i wake up
in the middle of the night
wishing i had a powerful message
i could share with the world

but then i go to record it
and no words come out

i believe a single whisper is enough to change the universe
this book is a whisper
shouting the beautiful things of life
from the balcony of your apartment
from the capitol building of every nation

as a hidden message
in every book that was ever written
every book that tried to portray the beauty of the soul
every painting and every note of every song

the only thing
i want to think about is what is here and now

today was my first day at this school
i walked down the halls and looked at your faces
but didn't say a word to any of you

there is a presence i want to feel
that is gone now
but resides like a ghost with me always
like the mist stays after the rain
how there is no evidence of a bird
once it flies through the air
i will write this entire book all in one night
the next day you will read it
and realize that when no one is listening
there is no connection
and therefore no resurrection

the best part about falling in love
is the life that comes from it
the best part about falling headfirst
into something you
are not prepared for
is the fact that you know you will take the dive

last year there was so much snow falling
that i stood in the cold
and school was canceled but
i walked outside and felt every part of the world

the air was freezing
the streets were covered
but i never felt so alive
even in that moment
when we were forced to stay
inside that entire day
and not go to school
and face
the people i knew would never understand me

i felt coldness
like many people feel love in every part of their body

sometimes i want to work and never stop working
never stop loving and never stop creating
but other times i find it so hard to get out of bed,
spending all day in the retail store

i do my best to make money with my own strength

one of the worst things in life
is losing someone close to you
but there is something even worse than that
losing someone who should have been close to you
but who you scorned and was never near to you
never finding your home
or falling into the arms of loved ones
but drifting through each place with no support
i imagine it is like this in many
of the countries i have never been to
today i weep for the loss of all of these things

2

when we are together
i know it will happen
you will hold me close to you
and the sparks will fly
and then we will leave each other
and dream about each other
and then we will feel a need to see each other
but won't be able to for whatever reason
and then there will be sadness for whatever reason
when the world falls apart
we won't be able to mend it
because we are on opposite sides of the world
and will spend the rest of our lives etching toward
the middle of the world
but will never reach it
and sew the world back together

3

some people have nothing to fall back on
we let them perish

4

it was a dull and dreary night
the clouds covered the stars
the clouds covered the moon
darkness covered the world

i was inside and took out my pen and paper
and wrote about what i saw
i heard the wind howling against my front door
and thunder crashing round

and then the power went out
and we sat in darkness for several hours
and then i was brought
into a world in which things were brighter

and then i was on a train, riding to a city
i had never been in before
and then i was working in an office as hard as i could
and years later my life was over
and i had spent my days doing nothing notable
or interesting enough to write down
and i have so many thoughts that are not interesting
enough to write down

i believe my words
will be forgotten soon after i am gone

5

the nature of beautiful and passing things

i was on a flight back to California,

the only sincere art comes from broken places
the computer i used to write all of these poems,
is now shattering across the floor,
the keys all strewn
and falling out

the broken things are what i am drawn towards

not just what they are
but the memory of what they were
and in my dream
we were lying in the autumn leaves
of the forest
the sky was growing darker because of the sorcerer
wielding his magic,
and the world was growing colder

but you gripped onto me
you led me out of the forest
and into the light of the city

we came to a junkyard covered in gasoline
and i was the one to light the flame
and the burning started
and did not stop

6

i have so much passion
i stayed up all night writing and reading
as many fantasy books as i could

nothing can stop the cascading years
nothing can stop the wrinkles on our hands

nothing can stop the glory of what we have already
and are about to experience

we both dread it and we love it

we become bonded in a communion

we dream about the worlds that we would experience
if only we were taking in each breath
with realization and then action

we will never

be left to our devices to be who we want to be

7

soon i will have changed so much
that even if you saw me

you will not recognize the person i will become,
after the years we were away

8

in less than an hour i filled the pages of that notebook
sometimes i feel lonely but it doesn't bother me

sometimes when i'm at work at retail stores
i stare at the ceiling
and think
and imagine my life in other countries
but now i am lying alone in my room
thinking about the world we created together
when we were kids
thinking about how much
we have grown in the past year
thinking about
the revival that will encompass our own lives
as the next year cascades into us

i had an entire binder of movies
and a shelf full of books
the same stories i would read over again
contemplating the nature of re-created things
and if there will be a re-creation
in my own life or yours
because there is so much doubt
and so many things we don't know about eternity
the one thing i want to do is leave this town and go
to a big city and see the skyscrapers
and then contemplate the same questions
and see if my answers have changed
but if my answers are not true

if not even with all wisdom in the world
can we find the nature of created things
and the nature of passing things
then how can we hope to know anything
about these things?
and if we don't know anything about these things
we are skydiving out of a plane
into an ocean
of regret, regretting the things we never did
regretting the things we did
regretting the chance we will never have
to grow into braver and honest persons
because no one could understand
the nature of self-sacrifice
but that is what it is like to be in the world

when the dusk turns to night,
i will contemplate these questions again
because yesterday was here but now is gone
now it is night but i don't want to sleep,
just want to stay up all night and dream
about places i could be but am not right now
about things i could be doing but will never do
about hands that would lift me out of the dark
but i will never see
about voices that would call me that i will never hear
and also about corporations
and governments that want
to destroy us
that want to take advantage of us
that see us as a means to an end
we live our lives in the world
as if these things did not exist
we live as if we are free
but we are really slaves
we dream as if
these shackles were not on our hands but they are
as we are alone in the prison you make me feel as
if we are walking
through fields of green and fields of light
where we not only comprehend

the beauty of the world
but also believe in it
and know it will take us out of this darkness
our lives are so linked
we are so connected in ways we do not admit
but know deep down in our hearts
and these links are not only fundamental to us
they guide us into the future
memories of you and me together as friends
overcoming our demons
i always dream
about traveling to vast, open, beautiful and magical worlds

9

you called my name but i was not there
i was traversing the forest of the world
i was enticed by the magic of it
i was listening to rock bands
and then i was once again staring
at the stars
all of them aligned the way they are supposed to be
and in my dreams my lips touched yours
i could feel the blood pulsing through your body

10

we are made up of broken pieces

i have memories of being alone in that city
smog covered the sky
the night covered the earth
i was reaching for someone to take my hand
and then i was on a plane
traveling far away from there
and i never thought of it until now
there's only one thing i am certain of
we are running out of time in the world
and there is no greater power
reaching down to take my hand
but at the same time

no one thinks about these things
we traverse through the world
learning more about it every day
yesterday i was alone in the classroom

i was the first to arrive
i was the last to leave
there is no one here that speaks my language

no one here thinking about tomorrow and not today

no one here dreaming about eternity
no one contemplating
the depths of what melody can do
and no one experiencing it
just a group of people
ignoring me when i speak to them
walking away when i approach them

all they say are words i will never hear

all we are is forces opposed to each other

but there was a blank page in front of me
i filled it with thirteen thousand words
in the period of one night
i didn't sleep at all
i just wrote

a metaphor in one place
clear and easy to understand words in another
but in all places truth

i want to write these words
all over the lockers of this school

and to broadcast them on every airwave
without saying a single word to anyone
words on a page will change the world
and i will never use my mouth to speak
these words will be like razor blades

they will pierce your skin
and the blood of the people will mix together
creating something new
there are so many voices in this room before the class
is about to start

i picked up a guitar
for the first time in a long time yesterday
and started to strum basic chords

i let the music take me over

all i wanted was to feel the grace
of confidence of a stable future

of a life lived with a purpose
there are souls dying to express what's inside of them
but they have no way to share it

i will be the voice
not only for those souls but for mine as well

remember the times we were walking
through the woods
and then walking by the lake
and then walking through the city
walking through the world
walking in the snow
walking in the light
walking in the night

in my dreams we were dancing together
in my dreams we were falling together
in my dreams there is motion in the world
in my dreams we are falling through eternity
and we understand its nature
and in those dreams i am begging you
to take me anywhere away from waking up
when i am asleep and dreaming
the world is not itself
what i need is a miracle

because during the day i call your name but no one can hear me

11

we were coasting through the world
we were watching the parts we love disappear
the memories of our loved ones
i was sitting on the bridge,
i was watching the water flow,
i was hiking across a mountain
i was waiting for you to come and rescue me
but then i realized i was never in need of saving
i long to have something for myself
something i can hold and never let go of
i mourn the loss of what i will never have
i am exalted in celebration for what i will always have
i long for things i will never understand
i can't see them but i know them
i can't feel them but i know them
i do not hear anyone
speaking about them but i know them
but i know that if i am alone with what i long for
i will never long for anything again
i go into the woods with a tape recorder
and start recording the spirits of the birds
the voices of the trees
and when i get home
i write down all of the lessons
that i learned from these things
in a notebook
and then i put them in a book and send it to you
you do not know these things but i know them,
the wind against my skin is enough to overpower me
and then i walk through the green fields
but do you believe in redemption?
do you know that it will win?
songs i never listen to echo in my mind

12

one love
the moments when you are alone
and
i am alone too
but we are in different countries
and you have not met me,
you stare at the lights on the ceiling
i am gazing at the open sky
contemplating the nature of
the truths we don't understand
but think about more than anything else
and later i dream
about being somewhere not one person
will find me
because no one finds me in my dreams,
because when i sleep i am alone
and forget i need anything at all

13

i feel as if in another life
i lived it entirely on the sea
watching the waves roar
dreaming that i would eventually
reach the shore
and in this life
which i no longer recall
i felt your breath against my neck
it might have been the wind
but it was strong, enthralling
and encapsulating of all things i
believed about myself and about love

when you see me,
what is it that you think
i am feeling, and thinking?

when you see me,
can you tell that my soul is real?

you fall in love
with what is in the soul,
you dream about other worlds with yours,
you fall into the depths
of emotions you would never feel yourself
when your soul is entrenched in mine
it stays there
and it doesn't ever need to leave,
> *what would make someone*
> *want to bully another person?*
> *to strike them down,*
> *to insult them,*
> *to steal,*
> *to lie,*
> *to abandon them*
> *in their desperate*
> *hour?*

i never understood it,
and i am being totally honest with you,
i feel so good whenever
i use my words to tell you how i feel
but no one is here to listen to my words
what are the things you will feel next
when you read my words?
nothing—or simply darkness,
inhabiting my poems,
imbibing themselves in
each syllable,
translated into your sighing and
freed by your tears,
the summer is so far away,

all we can feel is the overpowering
force of winter,
driving into us
and taking us to places we
don't want to be,
we all seem sad, in ways that
those around us did not understand,
when people walk by me, they just ignore me
i see darkness all around,
but it all exudes from my soul,
it will follow you
after you read these words,
to places you felt
you would never feel the shadow follow you

15

however, i can imagine what you are feeling,
and what is inside your soul,
i can fall headfirst into a dream
in which
i have become the person that you are

16

the sunset
and then the rain pouring down upon
this lonely planet,
where we do not have any idea
what happens to us after our deaths,
where we do not care much for anything
but books and routine,
rather than experiencing,
and feeling, and then dreaming
and then waking up
and repeating all of this in joyful motion

17

i dread the days when i grow older,
i know there will be days when
the world grows colder
and the air will be burning with freeze

18

taken far away from our homes,
and taken to a cage
where we will never escape,
where we starve to death
and no one cares for us again
because we cannot leave or use
our voices to call for help

19

i think i would like to live past my youth
and experience what it's like
to be 30 and then 40,
to have other
concerns than the ones i have now,
and to laugh about tomorrow,
what i cry about today,
i am missing the sensations i felt in
my youth,
i am falling forward into dreams again
and this time, i don't believe i'll wake up
at least not for several lifetimes
and my poetry books will sit on the shelf
of my room and then the shelf of a dusty
museum, until someone has the courage
to pick them up, blow the dust off
and discover for themselves
what i was feeling

20

at the party,
the students drink too much,
two students making out in the corner of the room,
and the music blaring
and i am in the back of the room with
my notebook writing this poem
all we crave is connection
but the kind that never dies,

21

i have fantasy books on the walls
of my room,
i come back to them whenever i want to feel
power or love or anything at all
different than what is here and now
i am taken far away when i think for a few
moments that there is truth
in the tales that are fantastical,
tales of faeries,
and dragons
but there are also shadows
where the vampires dwell,
they exist in our world too,
but they go by different names,
laying in wait for us
to attack us
and to manipulate us

22

i feel like i will be in this high school
forever,
just looking at your faces,
i am now sitting in homeroom
and i don't talk to anyone
but instead write this poem,
maybe one day we will speak,
maybe one day we will fall in love,

maybe we will fall headfirst after each other
maybe we will discover the truth
about what exists now, forever, and after
and also the things we know that will never last forever, or at
least we hope
that they will be destroyed
and never follow us after our deaths

23

i will write these lines
as you laugh about things i don't understand
and you will understand things
about me, when you read my words
that you would never, even until the end
of all time, know by simply looking at me

24

you are broken
i am too,
falling
into a routine
where there will be no change
in the world—
ever or at all

25

when i wrote letters,
i would pour my heart out
into those letters

26

you don't feel anything
everything is numb

27

turn up the music
and dance with me,
if you can hear me at all…

28

you have sewn the part of my heart
back together
that was broken when i realized
everyone dies for the first
of an infinite amount of times

29

the moon is bright and beautiful
you see it,
as i imagine we will walk outside
hand in hand,
you are my Pain,
the one whose hand i hold when
i don't remember
why i am here,
or what i was doing
except you remind me
that there is life
and i may never find you or
even understand your nature

30

i wish i could stay inside all day long
and contemplate things
and dream of things
and become one with the friction
and chaos of the world
when i write about both

31

there is destruction in the world
there once was something so beautiful
annihilated before its time,
and we can never get it back
or anything like it

32

the clouds are beautiful,
they are almost reachable
but not quite touchable
blood dripping down her wrists
when all she has is taken from her,
when we inflict torture on each other
with no savior,

33

i will write words
that will distress you
because you won't understand them
or understand if this darkness i write about
is real or really fictional

34

i open the doors to your prison
and guide you out
to a desperate and beautiful world

35

you will never realize what you took away
the world itself grows darker
with every passing day,
falling down the stairs headfirst into
the dark,
with a thousand needles sinking into your skin,
the walls that surround you

are caving in,
you know they would never listen even if
they could,
all the love in the world, now is gone
for good

36

everyone has an agenda
and love is rarely part of it

37

we are the youth
we are those uninvolved
we are those taken to where we never
wanted to go

38

i call your name,
you hear my name
but i sound dead
i hold your hand
you reach for it
but it feels cold
you drew me out of
myth and into the truth of expression

39

 the sound of the birds
carried by the breath of the wind
as the sunlight breaks through over
the bridge, through the trees
this is the moment i exist in now
soon it will vanish

40

when we find ourselves alone on hospital beds
you rush over to find me,
but i am gone before you reach out to me

41

there is a vibrancy that only exists
in human souls,
there is clarity when we look into
the eyes of another
i feel so much connection
to you when i go and inhale
the scent of the trees,
of these woods i walk alone in,
wishing i was not walking alone
wishing i could feel something like
the warmth of your hand
the depth of your sweat against my skin
the natural lights
it seems are a reflection of
a light i've never seen

42

when all i desire is unity
with the expressions of love
i have felt throughout
my fleeting days

when all i dream about is
to become so close to you
that i will never feel anything else again
when i tell you about love,
we will no longer describe it as something
we believe we may never attain,
when we come closer to each other,
we will be drawn and magnetized
and never pull away

43

i spend more days in my room
staring intently at the ceiling
studying it, and then blasting music
bands you've never heard of before

44

i can already hear them asking
"what was the point of all of Serenity's poems?"
the point was
so that when you are silently praying
and begging "god"
for "salvation",
that you can remember that you read
these poems,
and when you read these poems,
you will wish that the world slowed down
for just a moment longer,
so that you can tell the universe
or "god" or whatever you believe in
that you still want your lover
but she will never come back to you
because she took her last breath
long ago
and you are overcome by
a sudden feeling of dread
but still desperation,
not quite despair but it is a feeling
akin to it

i have more words to write,
you're not even close to the end
of this file yet,
you will read more words
about sadness and despair
hope and restoration
rebirth and then nothing more

45

stay with me
for tonight at least
and i will read all of these words
and your mind will be transformed
your heart will be changed,
and salvation will come
to another one of the lost sheep of the world,
the wolves in the field won't find you
you will become so close to me
and our friendship will lift us out of
this world
together, for a long time, if not forever

46

you were not here for me
when i cried out with a shrilling voice
in the middle of the dark,
you were not here for me
when melody was inside my soul
and you didn't know what it was
so you threw it away and it shriveled up
and died
and my heart never had a song inside it again

47

the music is loud,
the band takes the stage,
telling us more about ourselves
than we ever told our friends

48

poets from a far off land
will meet here
at a reading
but none of their words
have the power that mine have

none of them will write about
anything that i am feeling now

49

there was a distant land
in a different time
than the one we have grown so familiar with
in this land
there was always a shadow overcoming it
but when the days of darkness
ended the people came out of the
holes they dug for themselves
and became one with the sunlight

50

falling in love
with poetry
when i am alone on my bed,
and then the cosmos resonates
and it speaks to me
and tells secrets to my soul
that you would only hear if you listened
closely and felt my breath

51

the moment when we spend all our days
inside our own home
reading books about religion
and philosophy
because we believe
if we study these works for long enough
our lives will be transformed
and we will all become new persons
longing for the light underneath the entrance to the juvenile
detention center
i hear stories about kids who have
done terrible things
and they want their sins to be forgiven,

how hatred and death follow us all
and some of us have not even done a thing
wrong, but through the darkness
our voices eventually grow silent
and when no one hears them
there will be a resonance
that shatters through
the dire moments
when we need you more than ever,
and right now i crave salvation
now more than ever
salvation from the decadence
in the summer of when the firestorm
destroys our home
and later on the shackles are unlocked
and clatter onto the floor
and we follow the prison guard
out of the juvenile detention center
and into the dark world
where we struggle each day to get someone
to understand the truth
about the torture
in our hearts that claws us
until we collapse
and when we collapse we might never stand up again
the song in a minor key,
ominous, clairvoyant, beautiful,
enchanting
hearkening death
and prophesying life,
all at the same time,
we are begging to be saved from
what we don't understand,
i am imploring you,
take me far away from this school
where i will never be loved or known by
anyone,
a few days later i will stand naked
in front of the mirror,
stepping out of the shadow
my eyes seeing in the mirror

what i will never understand
and you know too
that you will never understand me
or grasp me,
complicated thoughts in my mind,
i fall in and out of love all of the time
what i say i don't really mean,
when the embers in the night
burn they never go out but are never seen
they light our path anyway,
even though we cannot see them,
despite their dimness,
they follow us like fireflies
and we only believe
in the things we see with our own eyes
but sometimes
we don't believe our eyes either,
i am somewhere walking over the edge of the
bridge and my Pain is walking with me,
the dying wish in my broken heart,
to fall so deeply into an ocean of
despair, that hope will eventually
pull me up and i will stand on my own two feet
and eventually return to the land
from which i was taken
and then talk to those in the land of despair
and tell them about the colors,
the lights,
the tastes, the smells,
the love, the charity
of a beautiful but broken world
that none of them were brave enough to
experience again
i will lift them up and take them with me
to a place where they will never desire
to go anywhere else again
it is always better to feel
than to feel nothing at all

52

in my dreams,
            you are
                                    here
you
            believe

in what is pure and true
you wish you could travel through time
and find yourself in the arms
of a lover, who left your life long ago

there are demons in this world
there are angels in this world

life hurts in this world
i want to leave this world
but i cannot tell the angels from the demons
or the light from the darkness
or the difference between torture
and tranquility,
when confusion is all that fills this world

53

i am falling deeper
into the fits of depression
no one ever understood
if they understood these things
we would know what to call them
and if we knew their names,
we could tell them to leave us forever

54

i asked for help,
you weren't there
you told me never
to talk to you again

55

love drifting across my skin like water
when you touch me,
you grip me and put your arms behind my neck
chemicals in our minds
telling us this is right,
that despite those who would find us
we know what we are doing is right,
the chemicals in our minds
were wiser
than the voices of dissention
because they've been here some trillion years
existing in the universe
before any of us ever existed

56

you and i coming home together
i've never experienced this
but i can imagine what it would feel like
and the bliss of when the world
is in passion
and when love is in motion
and then love rests
when you and i are together
and all of the doors of us are closed
to everyone, except to each other
you can come to me
and find anything you need

57

at the frat party
the hip hop music
blaring from the speakers

of this home where people lived
and moved out
stories told and then forgotten

"Serenity" says someone approaching with a beer bottle in hand

"have a drink with me"

i'm not interested
i leave and walk
away, walk home in the cold
and on my journey home, i meet people
we both believed to be dead
i converse with them and imbibe my words
into their floating spirits

58

a year ago all that summer
i worked at a catering company
i would attend those weddings
and serve food at the reception
and i felt content
in the fact
that i could make other
people happy
even though i was never paid for that job
at all
because the company went out of business
before they could pay me
i had a dream
about being in another universe
and
i am trying to call you
but the number never reaches you
and at this moment i am walking through
the woods
again for the one hundredth time this year
i feel the most at peace when
the sunlight breaks through the trees
and i can feel the warmth on me
and i can feel the emotions swelling up in
nostalgia, telling us all about our past lives

59

if we could come back from the dead,
we would fill the world with words
about how fleeting our lives are now

when our families are broken,
and we wander the empty streets
without a home,
we shiver in the cold
and not one person hears our voices,
in the shrill of the night

60

i had a dream that we went on a long trip together,
across the country

i had a dream that when we listened for the voice of god,
we could hear that voice clearly
and that voice told us
the secrets we never admitted about ourselves

i had a clear vision that
when we were falling deeper, drowning in the Atlantic
there was something to lift us out
and to get us to cough up all of the water
and then breathe the free air again
and walk the earth for another eighty or so years

i had a dream that
you looked very different than you do now
and we were listening to songs
we would never listen to
and we learned to live life
to its entire extent

i have a memory that poems are always
true
and they tell us all the truths
we know are true

but never admit to another soul

61

i held the manuscript in my hands
but no one saw it and i locked it away and never
touched it again

62

when i think of
the poverty
that is in the world
i realize that no
one is thinking about it
because there
is no way to
stop it from taking over,
so that from
one moment on
we live with nothing
and when we have nothing
we still will have the love
of our family
and then we don't care
about any material things

63

through the devastation
we walked all along the outskirts of the world

through the times when we were better off dead than alive
we clung onto our lives
like they were very beautiful and
they meant more to us
than the torture we were feeling

64

the vastness
of the oceans
and how we will never
swim too far from the shore
and in nations faraway,
there are people like us,
near their shore
swimming in the ocean,
wondering about the nature
of the sky
and the reason there are countries
with borders at all
when all the borders do
is keep us separated from
understanding
and after we walk back from the beach,
we go to a tavern
and eat cheesesteaks together
and you talk about the time
that has passed
and the friends we lost years ago,
while i listen intently
and then you
talk about the poverty that is in the world
and i cannot believe
what has happened to the world
and there are no other worlds
if we lose the one we have
and i fall asleep that night
alone and dream that there are other
worlds
and that in them there is magic
in desperation,
hope thriving in suffering
and that is the world where we sit
on the beach and watch the mermaids
swim in the ocean, by the shore
and they spray and souse us
and then we understand

the nature of connection,
of friendship and of passing
and valuable things

65

there is a rhythm
that keeps us in motion
from day to day
if we pretended that this day
was our last day,
we would not spend it any
differently
i could become like Elena Gilbert,
taken into a tidal wave
of dark magic
and then overcome
by the same melody that comes from
this magic
and totally enthralled by it,
fall into the arms of a
lover who should have been dead,
because truth be told,
both of us should have been dead,

but then suddenly there is
salvation,
and i am human
i am alive with my lover
and then we can be together
forever.

i could be Denna
and my lover could be Kvothe,
we could live in a land
where there are trials
adversity, wealth
but also ignorance,
and i, Denna, will fall headfirst
into you,
not wanting anything else but

to be loved forever and after,

and in another universe i'm like Angel
and my lover is like Buffy
only in the fact
that you must let go of me,
because loving me
does nothing but cause you torment
but at the same time,
the only thing we will ever desire
is eternal life,
but we never drink from the cup of
salvation
we never eat the bread of life
but instead eat from the table
of our own despair and our own wanting
and needing and then
our own deaths,
these deaths will be short and sweet
these moments will drown us
in their own music
an enchanting melody but one we
will never understand
and it is as dangerous as it is lovely

and it is as desperate as it is sure,

and we know what we long for
but we never name it
we know what we taste in our mouths
but we never keep that taste,
we know what it is to be in love
but we only have one word for
it in the English language

today i sit in front of the locker
and all of these words flow from my pen
today i sit in front of my locker
you are quite oblivious to me
you are quite unknowing of
the things i know you will never understand

it is important to try
to understand
even if you know you never will understand

i dyed my hair pink a few days ago
because i wanted to tell
you that i don't want to fit in
i never will
i must stand out from the crowd and be
remembered
as the only one who dressed or acted
a certain way,
but i will sit in the back of the room,
and i will be totally relaxed
but never at peace
always at war with the world
always trying to find an excuse to become
a little bit stronger in this conflict

66

oh my dear,
you know that when we meet
there will be fireworks
i can imagine what will happen
the first time that we kiss,
the first time we fall in love,
the first time we are together,
the first time you hold me
and try never to let go,
but we must leave for one or other reason
but now you will always be here
in these words,
can you leave these words?
no. you are enshrined here together
with me
and we are dancing
and laughing whenever these words
are read
and we wait here for someone
to read these words,
until they are read, then nothing happens

67

today we wait
as the hunger inside us grows
for the kind of fulfillment
we will never have
we dance in our own dreams
with friends we will not
be friends with in our lives
words on the pages of these notepads
soon to come alive,
while people across our borders
are alienated,
we stay inside our walls
and write
stories of our own
a trip to the beach,

you and me alone in your car,
when we reach the beach, i am exonerated
and spin around, with my arms outstretched
i am grasping at truth
and i dream of being held in the arms of you, my lover

68

how can we describe torment and misery?
what would bring someone to the moment of anguish?
we can dream about being so far away from each other
that we meet each other on opposite sides,
and then stick to each other and are never again separated

69

as long as there are dreams which we share,
so joined together and which we grasp so tightly
we will have this connection,
chiefly, when you dream about traveling the world
and i dream about it too,
with each year that we grow older,
you understand more about the world
secondarily when we hold on to memories
only you and i have shared together

every year when our birthday came,
we would find ourselves clinging onto the years
that were fleeting,
drifting deep away from a world that was needing,
to realize its own desperation,
and we were truly free in our own expression
when no one could tell us to stop writing,
singing, expressing and growing
and loving and thriving and feeling

the passing days have drifted us apart,
we live separate lives, we speak, once a day,
then once a week and then once a month
but i know you will find life in my poems
the best friend i've ever had

with a heart that is growing old
and also growing warmer,
opening up to the world,
seeing the lights and the beauty
that is only comprehended when you stop
and take in several very deep breaths
and then you stop and realize
that the act of breathing
is the reason why we are alive,
love pulling our cells together
while entropy tries to tear us apart,
today is our birthday again and i think about you
though you are on the other side of the country
but though we walk different paths
i am convinced they all lead back to where they started
                your friend forever   -Serenity

70

we are alone in dark rooms,
we hear music telling us
that there once was a time when we thrived
in the bright and open world

71

as the nights
drift on,
we fall asleep
and are carried away
far out to sea
on ships that have never touched our shore

72

we grow closer
to wanting to fall in love
each day
with feelings we
will never express again
because we cannot define any of these

feelings,
we become emancipated
by the time we've sacrificed
serving others
and falling away from our own dreams
and then those ships where we lay
asleep never approach the shore
we called home ever again

73

from the steeples of the church
and the faces of those nameless in the crowd
passerby, abiding here only for a short time
until they drift away into the depth of music
and here i am contemplative
feeling for all things
expressing all truth
and becoming closer to mortality
hearing the music which the crowd is drawn by myself
and then i drift into the crowd
and become myself—entranced by the music like all others
and then i follow its rhythm
and am lost, am forgotten, am drifting into
universes where we become easily replaceable

74

the first day i saw you,
you never answered me,
so i drifted away from you
and never spoke to you again

and then i saw you
every day in classrooms
where there was a school i never attended
because i was only dreaming
now you are not part of my story
but you were part of a brief experience

75

the pressure laid down on our shoulders
prevents us from relaxing for a single moment
because this anxiety follows us

76

we stand on the national mall lawn and i kiss you,
we stand in places where we grow
and learn more about the world together
and this learning brings understanding
when the clouds grow dark
we stand underneath them
and i kiss you in the middle of the storm,
when the news arrives that the war has just begun
i kiss you in the midst of the firestorm
when we are desperate to be heard,
we give our love that we created together freely to the rest of the
world, and as the world receives this love
it learns more about itself than i could ever teach it

77

i hear you walk by
you sing
"kiss me
and take off your clothes"
you were lying in bed next to her
she was singing softly and quietly
while she was in love
"kiss me and
take off your clothes"
when we grow so close
that all we can think about
is being with our own girlfriends
and you hold her,
and then when you are not holding her
you count down the days
until
you see her again

and then you feel so
passionate when you meet again,
you cannot describe what you are feeling
but my words will come so close to describing it
there is something deep in our bones
that brings us together
bonds unbreakable, truth
unforgettable,
every single night when we labor
presumably in vain in a dead end job
but then we come home, and you fall asleep
on the couch alone, remembering the days when there
were books worth of stories to tell about the love we feel when
we are
joined close

today
i long for all of the things i felt in my past

78

the light on my face warming it up
gives me strength, comfort
understanding and faith
that each day will follow the other
and as these days pass the cycle of creation
will go on for an eternity
while we patiently wait for the days of summer to set in,
and then we
embrace the freedom in the summer with open arms
and we explore the vibrant parts of the world
we fall in love and discover some of the things we were lacking

79

when you think of the summer
while you are alone in your room
and the snow covers your streets
you remember love found and then lost
how you would fall asleep on the couch
with her and run your fingers through her hair

before you both would fall asleep
you feel surrounded by warm nostalgia
you feel enveloped in the tantalizing motions
of the things you will never experience again

when i stand in the snow and i shiver
i dream about the days when the summer heat would
strike my cheeks and the warmth itself would fill me with peace
when i stood on the beach with my friends
until the sun went down
and this would go on for three months
until the routine of school would start again

80

in our youth
we were so excited to be in the world

as the days passed
we became used to the sights we saw
and the gorgeous and vibrant world
had suddenly become mundane to us
because we were so used to seeing
the rivers and mountains and the trees
we will never feel the same way about the world since when
it was new to us
and we also discovered
that there can be places within human hearts
where there is no charity,
that turns a cold shoulder to the beggar at their doorstep
that takes what never belonged to them
destroying life and love
but through the passing years
we have learned to fight for what is right
to welcome those in need
and to be a friend to those who have nowhere else to turn

81

we are coasting through a world that has become chaotic,

when the ones you love are suffering
you give and never stop,
you are always there
for the people that you love

despite the chaos in this world
you greet each day with a smile
and hold your head up high

82

she broke up with you because she
believed you cheated
rumors spreading like wildfire
none of them were true
it hit you like a heart attack when she left
you couldn't believe it was happening
so sudden, so cruel, so desperate
to express how you felt
and now she is with someone else
you were so close,
promises broken
the love that was supposed to be forever
but we forgot what forever means
at night you lie alone at home
you are serenaded by the dial tone,
and then you stop calling
and never think of her again
because we forgot the meaning
of forever.

83

you are a light that reminds me
that there is
a path that leads away from routine,
that takes me to

places where the world will never be dull
you are the warmth
that fills me with joy
and knowledge
that love is tangible,
and powerful enough to overcome
what we believed
was insurmountable
and when i kiss you
i feel overflowing with peace
as if all the broken pieces
in the world had been reconciled
and as the years pass
there will be
a million more ways
to fall in love with you
all over again

84

my guitar is broken
and i never picked one up
again

i will stay inside listening to
Beatles songs
wishing i could write songs
or that anyone would listen to the words i write

85

it feels like betrayal
        when
i come to you
        and you swear to tell no one
                but you lie

the darkness
that was hidden in the vastness of this world
calls to us,
telling us
that we are
beyond saving,
coming to us like music comes to us,
coming to us in our despair like death
in the thick of conception

today we wait by the dark abandoned city
and the light of moving feet
will never grace these streets again,

we walk through the midst of the riots
this night on the fourth of july
in Chicago
after the fireworks,
we all implode and reach a breaking point

i have dreams about being far away from
the city
and becoming someone and breaking
far away from poverty

and then a new melody befalls us
as we walk back to the airport,
telling us to never come back to this same city ever again

when i needed you,
you were never there for me
and i was dying without your help
and then resentment grew until i was dead

what a joy it is to be alive,
but in death we find ourselves closer to
becoming something we never knew we would become
so close to nothingness
we can taste our own nonconception,

we can forget that we were staring at the ceiling
wondering why we were alive
and then we will go to different cities and read passionate words
to strangers
that will change and transform the world
slowly, a person at a time

> when your heart beats close to mine,
> our fears flee quickly from us
> when the night grows dark
> and the siren song calls to us
> and our ship draws closer to that dreadful shore
> we hold on to what is precious to us
> my hand falls naturally into yours
> i believe all things will be made right
> somewhere before the end
> anywhere
> like the kingdom of light
> encompassing
> the world

while the fools
are guiding the world to where it will
never be the same again

we have so much
we are losing so much

the world is dragged through the mud
and this was the one world we had
the one life we had to live,
i miss being able to hold you whenever i wanted to

we follow the ocean on our journey
and let the stars guide us
as the wind is on our backs
as it takes several months
to reach our destination

we never understand the nature of time,
how things so far from us are now close to us
and then these things are gone far away from us

and we stand alone in
the darkness of the world
waiting
for the keys to be struck on the keyboard
to write the end of our story
and the ending of the story surprises us

today is all we have

my lover comes back to me
the sweetest hello
the saddest goodbye,
where my only desire is to remain with him forever

too often we forget
too often we do what is wrong
and then we fall into the depth of the night
into arguments and hatred
and we forget about our only desire,

desperate and hopeless,
alone and desolate,
getting off the bus at this city,
feeling the breathless cold
begging you to make a sound
that no one will hear
poetry no one will imbibe
depth that nothing will penetrate
        days where we lay alone
        looking at the distant stars
        remembering your hand slipping into mine
        remembering that we are the last of our own kind

as the night
becomes encompassed
in the storm,
you stay inside your hotel room
and never leave

we become so in love with all the feelings we will never
grasp or understand

we meet and talk about religion,
and magic and fantasies of the way the world
would be if only we were the ones who created the world
and we come together at times when everyone else is fighting

and love is broken so easily that we fall apart
and never wake up from the coma; we see the world
as a prison
which we have fallen into by mistake

we pretend that our families are still alive
and that when we say their names
someone in this universe hears those names

we lie to ourselves when we say
that creation will last forever
and that any one person will hear any of our words

i am the poet of all times,
i am the poet of the soul
and the poet of voiceless
because my voice has been taken from me as well
and i understand what the voiceless are going through

it is better to experience than it is to understand
it is better to feel the healing motions
than to never be wounded
but when language is exhausted
there will be no way to mend these wounds
when we stop understanding each other,
there will be no way to find the other anywhere
because we put up walls no one can penetrate
when we forget the meaning of truth
because we are penetrated by nothing
and we understand nothing

if you ever can feel the depth of what melody is,
beyond the pure chemicals in your mind
you will possess all knowledge

and i can imagine many things
as i sit in this classroom
actively not listening
to the teacher,
actively not paying any attention
to the students,
i will write about these stories
in this notebook

dreams of love lost in summers
forgotten
feelings inside clawing on our hearts
from the inside and tearing through
reaching through our bodies
and penetrating others

until the whole world
writhes in the same misery
and then realizes that it has
achieved the greatest anguish that could ever exist,
the way i felt with you,
like feeling things
i never believed could be felt within the human heart

the nature of creation
is too cyclical,
we are born,
we go off into the world
and we return to the dust
and become ashes and float across
the rivers

"Serenity,
remember there are many
memories you will make in
the future,
you can let go of the past"
he said to me, expecting me to understand

there are many things
i do not understand
and some things i am sure
i will never understand

when you tell me about the places you have gone to
i tell you i will never go to any of those places
but i will be walking through this city,

watching the smog cover the clouds
and watching the hellfire of the war
rain down on a lonely city

i want to find myself somewhere far from this city,
but will never

no one is there to greet me,
in these hallways,

shivering, freezing,
desperate, absolutely alone
no one would be listening
even if they could
like an episode of *the twilight zone*

i would never believe the world
would become like this
until the clouds covered the stars
until the smog covered the clouds
and until the redness of the firefight
covered the smog
filling the air with explosions
not like those of fireworks
but instilling fear and death in our hearts

the pictures have all grown so black and white
the color is taken from the world
and we don't remember what the
world looked like at all
when there was color in it
we will be scavenging to survive
and dreaming about
the way the world was before
the worst imaginable turmoil

we grasp onto
the words we hold close to our hearts
hoping they will bring us back to life
after we have passed away

we both remember
the way the world was,
when there was peace
and nothing could hurt us

you fall down into the night
and i dive after you

i am saved by the motion of the
water pushing me back to where i came from

the current takes me
back to my home
and then i forget about you
that you ever existed
and i wait for you to come back
because i am too afraid to dive after you
again

the ground slips out from under me
and i fall after you
and the current of the waves
cannot stop me from being submerged

but then we realize this was all just one dream,
and that i never met you
and that i've been longing to be with you
for my entire life
and we are lost in the depth
of the melodies we never understood

and after we woke up
we had to go back to school,
back to work
to live in a country surrounded by poverty
we wrote fifty books
during the course of our lives
but not one single soul read any of them
and these books contained the answer
that would eliminate poverty,
eliminate cancer
and alleviate but not completely blot out
the problem of death
and we forgot our own despair
and grasped onto hope

the peace we found
after we forgot our despair
was unimaginable
and perfect and pure,
we fell into the abstract concept
of truth

and lost ourselves in its dark night
where we did not know anything
except for what was true
we were lied to so much
that the light of truth was so small
we could barely see a thing
but we followed the light out of the tunnel
and into the deep and vibrant world

we dreamed about finding ourselves
in places we lived in
when we were only children

we dreamed that we never slipped
and fell down a flight of stairs
into the darkness
of an abandoned subway station
where we lay motionless
for several days until someone
crawled down into the hole after us
and took us to a hospital

we didn't want
to be separated so we stitched
our dreams together
so that when we ran after these dreams
we would end up finding each other in the end

we fell deeply in love
with these dreams that were so close
and then our destinies were sealed with each other

you promised me that we would never settle for anything else
but an eternity searching and finding
what the poets had written about forever

        we take off down the highway
in your car and we discover everything we were lacking
in the moments when the world slows down
in traffic
in the moments when we walk through the forest

and fall into each other's arms
not thinking about the rest of our life
or any other moment but this single present moment

but really i am still sitting in this hallway of this school
writing about everything i see
as the first day of this school year is about to end
and we hear the clattering noise of feet against the floor
and the banter of gossip, indistinguishable from
any other words
as we hear the names of people who died last summer
the names of celebrities
who we will never meet
the names of bands,
whose concerts i never attended
songs i never sang,
but all of these things will be sung in this poem,
all of these will thrive in the life of poetry
where actions are enshrined

i will be your heroin,
i will be your ecstasy
more than an illusion
something you will never forget
when we understand how quickly we are drifting
how quickly our hearts are fading,
your heroine
your only lover from a world you do not understand
i am not from this world,
and i can take you out of it,
take you far from where we are now
and thought we would be forever

listen carefully as i tell you all the secrets about yourself
you weren't brave enough to admit to yourself
you're a liar,
you're a thief,
you're a cheater,
but it doesn't matter when we all are drifting
we are now totally numb to all the things
that bothered us before,

after we lose our lives

take my hand now

      take my heart now

bind our lives together now,
take my virginity now

      make our blood become one now
so that we can be taken out of this world
and into the new and exciting world

your hand in mine we will walk through these walls
and never return here again. we will
be doing what the others were dreaming of doing for their entire
lives
we will be what they dreamed

we wanted a new life our whole lives
now is our chance to
      stitch the broken pieces
          we had become
                  into one
    single
           new
and whole piece
now is our chance to destroy the fear

i am compelled to do what is right
by a force i do not understand

i want to take you with me
when we discover new worlds

i want to take you with me
when we discover truth
about ourselves
that no one else has ever understood
when we keep expressing
and never stop expressing
when we keep breathing
and never stop breathing
when we find what is beautiful about
each other and never stop loving each other
when we find what we longed for as kids
and watch the time drift away
until we are no longer children
and watch the time drift away
until we are old and in our deathbeds
and we explored so much of the world
that we knew every crevice
and crease of the world,
and could feel not only the dirt but the nature of the sunlight
and we became certain
of these things,
so certain in fact that we were able to walk on the water without
second guessing
you were so certain that you took my hand without a second
thought, without doubting that i would reach out and let you
take my hand in yours
and you knew that peace was only a few moments away
in the voice of the poor people
in the voice of strangers you meet on the street
and lie about not having any money
and lie about not having any way to help those struggling
living on nothing to two dollars an hour
living your life in a shell you will never be able to escape from,
dreaming that there are better ways
to live our lives than to shut ourselves

off from the rest of the world
which is always reaching out to us
telling us that there are more places to explore in it
telling us that we are now forgetting the plans we had
years ago
and finding someone new to fall in love with
finding someone who will always love us unconditionally
and falling into an ocean where we will always reach out,
our head barely breaking through the water and seeing
the bright and blue sky
but we don't have enough strength to wade in the water
before the ocean overtakes us
and we slip into the water forever,
and then are reincarnated
into a new person and come into the world with a new name
and greet the world with opens arms,
unlike you did in your past life
and you forget the good things in life
because you know what life can
be like when you are rejected by everyone
and you come alive
and then you forget about what it was like
to want and need
and then you thrive

the music of the world
gets louder
and glasses are raised,
but we realize that your hand will not always be in mine

we are so far from what you wanted the world to be
but so close to perfection
and it is unthinkable how many emotions you feel,
reaching a breaking point,
reaching a boiling point
love the world will never comprehend
if i fall you run to catch me
and i do the same for you
        we can be the rulers
of a world that thought it had forgotten
its rightful king

if i leave and my heart grows colder alone,
        when you are not here
you will be on another planet
and then we struggle to find each other again
and there will be wars waged across the stars
and there will be
death that follows all of us
until we understand
that we cannot escape from it
and lie down on the grass
and feel the dew on it
and let the water transform you into a new creation
and then you sink deeper into the river
until you fall across the waterfall

come and greet me in the next light after the world
has awoken from a thousand years of night

come and greet me in the next song
after the world forgets how to sing for a thousand years

we are comprised of broken pieces
that will never come together except in the arms of each other

we are comprised of songs
we have forgotten
but will only remember the day
we are driving down the highway
without a care in the world
and will sing these songs like anthems

and these anthems will awaken the world
from the coma,
from the nightmare
it wanted to escape from but had fallen so deep into

how do i explain
the things i cannot explain to myself?

how can you expect to understand
any of the things
i have internalized
and know so closely
and contemplate every day
but do not understand even now?

how can you be so close to someone
and feel them as a part of you
but then have them torn from you forever?

what is the purpose of a life unlived?
how can we be so carried away with thoughts
of the life we have not yet understood?

where would you rather be than here?
i would rather be nowhere except for where i am now
this is the right place for me to be
scribbling words
on the broken pages of a notebook
that no one will ever see

words that everyone deserves to see

when we are about to conceive ideas
about the bright and glorious world
that will make us understand it
these words don't come out of our minds
and they are never expressed
in a true way

88

the emotions i have are so strong
that i write the same poem over and over again
expecting it to express what i feel in the clearest way
possible but nothing will express any of these things
except for repeating the word
over and over again

salvation

89

we run through the night
beside the broken road
and we never stop
until our hearts stop
wanting

90

passion
burning
thriving
living inside
breaking through
and breaking free
finding its place in an open
world that had forsaken
and forgotten it

91

pop songs at the dance
blaring from the speaker
we all do not want to be here

92

tear down your walls and let the love flood in

93

i see the band on the stage,
they understand me better than any lover

94

cutting my heart
how hard it is to thrive in worlds
where we do not understand anything
but misery we walk into and never
leave
i fell asleep in the car
i woke up in a different
city,
you do not understand
any of my poems

95

as our lives speed past us
we dream about being in the arms
of family
on the night we take our last breaths

i step onto that bus
and ride it and never return to this city,
ever again,

96

come and find me
come inside me
and never leave me

97

i will stay in my room
and read more fantasy novels
and understand more about the real world
than i would discover by reading any textbook

98

through my eighteen years
        i have changed so much,
i have loved so much
i have forgotten so much
i have become one with so many of the feelings
i thought i would never experience for myself
and i thought i would only sit back and watch other people
experience these things

99

the lights flashing as we drive through
the city at night once again
and i am falling asleep
and we hear the cries in the city of broken families
of those with no money,
of the riots starting to begin
of the days when we are afraid of losing everything

when all of the beautiful colors are now stale
when nothing tastes sweet
when nothing feels smooth, but only feels rigid
when we are freezing so much that we can barely move
and it hurts to move
when we are hurting so much and there is no one to tell how
much we are hurting to

100

we forget about what is true

101

morphine in your veins
you cannot feel anything at all
including the love i have for you

numbness worse than death

102

oh my dear,
come to me
when i am
in love with you
before i have forgotten you
when we are bursting with passion
and not indifference
depth and never despair
life and truth collide
when we touch
believe what i say,
that for so long
we have been suffering
in the midst of
the coldness
of a broken world
where tears are the only things
that fall from our eyes
where death is the only certain future event
where we are locked in an abandoned bathroom
with no way to get out

where we are locked inside
our own writings
and never are understood by anyone

and then we walk out into the world
and are ignored

103

i have been struggling to put my thoughts to words
for several years
but finally learned to write poems
and learned to not stop writing
to write through the dark clouds
until i can see through the clouds
and see the sun shining through these clouds

we will fall so in love that we will understand
truth and believe it too

you will be the voice inside my head
in a memory that i do not understand

you are a thief,
stealing my desire to live an ordinary life

we will never be comfortable with anything less
than passion
and perfection taking the place of bliss

when you see me
you stand underneath the street light
and we kiss for the first and the last time
and never understand why
but we know why
and then we fall down into the ocean
pure anticipation for what will happen next
we fall into the depth
of the lights of cities we will never visit again
i wish i could write more
and describe every detail of everything that i see
right now i can smell the marijuana

and i see the cars going by at the street light
and i see those lined up outside the club
waiting to get in
and when they get in they will hear loud music
and they will dance until their dreams
are following them home and into their beds
i have so many things to say
about this fragile but unbroken world

i have so many things to say
about my once whole but broken life

as the months go by i know we will feel so much
we will inhale so much
not just the drugs
but also the melodies
we find on the street corner
in the radios of the passing cars
and these melodies float up
into the air and reach the clouds
and travel to other cities
where there is someone like me
who understands me
and hears the same song and dreams about the same things
i dream about
when she falls asleep
and maybe in her dreams we will meet each other
if there was ever such as a thing
as one consciousness reaching out to another
but i find it so hard to believe any of this
but i believe it all
with the entirety of my broken heart
the tears will tell the truth
that every dream we believe will be attainable
like when you reach out for my hand
and i let you take my hand
and when you take my hand it sinks deep into yours
and then finds itself comfortable
and surrounded by truth
and then surrounded by love

we are slipping through the universe
we are once surrounded by love
but ultimately surrounded by nothing
we lock ourselves in rooms
where there are no songs
to be heard

104

sing the anthems with me
we are both slipping through the universe
and we sing together
we sing when we walk out of that classroom
and i grasp your hand
and you take it
and then we dance and are so content
and then you have so much energy
that you believe that nothing can stop you
from
becoming something more
than
who you appear to be,
you whisper to me,
you tell me all of your fears
and all of your dreams
you touch me
and it is perfect
you look at me
and you understand
and our souls almost touch but not quite

105

tongues expressing
the words
that were written on the page
and verbalizing,
speaking, vocalizing
what was never read before

the world
is enchanted by a shroud
that steals the light away from the world
covers the clouds
steals away the light
and breaks the beautiful things

107

not one person greeted me today
and i know that this is the way
the world will be for the rest of this year

today i feel so alone,
today i feel so tortured
that i could not undo what
has been done
that i could not feel enough for the people
who we live together with in this same world
that we cannot hold each other so close
that we can understand
what the soul is

the soul is never understood
and will never be grasped
or touched
by definition
we can get close to it
but it was never tangible
i always wanted to understand you
just a little but from outside
of the shell of the body
and to hold you and never let go of you

i will never change
i will always be the person that i am
no one can make me stop
i will always be held in the arms
of the breeze
of the free and open world
i will always be held in the arms
of a world that has forgotten more about itself
than it had ever learned
we are falling into the depth of despair
and we
no longer accept things we know to be unequivocally true
when the fire rains down from the sky
and the bombs go off
and then we don't feel a thing ever again
come closer and hold me
so i will never stop feeling you

Joseph Leo Hickey lives in Virginia. He is the author of *Baptism of Apathy*, *Unity*, *Love Poems at the End of Our Lives*, *Liefie*, *The Last Poem* and *Purity: Redeemed*. He is the founder of Melodium House.

YouTube: allthestarsaredead

www.ingramcontent.com/pod-product-compliance
Lightning Source LLC
LaVergne TN
LVHW051704080426
835511LV00017B/2714

*9 7 8 1 9 5 1 2 9 8 0 3 6 *